Cat-titudes to Live By

rachaelhale

HARVEST HOUSE PUBLISHERS

EUGENE, OREGON

Cat-titudes to Live By

Text copyright © 2008 by Harvest House Publishers
Published by Harvest House Publishers
Eugene, Oregon 97402
www.harvesthousepublishers.com

ISBN 13: 978-0-7369-2202-9
ISBN 10: 0-7369-2202-4

© Dissero Brands Limited (New Zealand) 2008
   All worldwide rights reserved.
      www.rachaelhale.com

Design and production by Garborg Design Works, Savage, Minnesota

Harvest House Publishers has made every effort to trace the ownership of all poems and quotes. In the event of a question arising from the use of a poem or quote, we regret any error made and will be pleased to make the necessary correction in future editions of this book.

Scripture verses are taken from the HOLY BIBLE, NEW INTERNATIONAL VERSION®. NIV®. Copyright©1973, 1978, 1984 by the International Bible Society. Used by permission of Zondervan. All rights reserved.

Printed in China

08 09 10 11 12 13 14 15 / LP / 10 9 8 7 6 5 4 3

Sense shines with a double luster when it is set in humility. An able, yet humble man is a jewel worth a kingdom.

WILLIAM PENN

humb

3

attitude

Our attitudes control our lives. Attitudes
are a secret power working twenty-four
hours a day, for good or bad. It is of
paramount importance that we know how
to harness and control this great force.

TOM BLANDI

True ambition is not
what we thought it was.
True ambition is the
profound desire to live
usefully and walk humbly
under the grace of God.

BILL WILSON

ambition

Far better it is to dare mighty things, to win
glorious triumphs, even though checkered
by failure, than to take rank with those poor
spirits who neither enjoy much nor suffer
much because they live in the gray twilight
that knows not victory nor defeat.

THEODORE ROOSEVELT

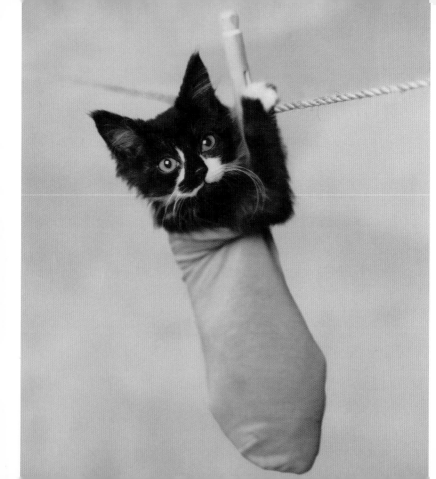

God provides the wind, but man must raise the sails.

SAINT AUGUSTINE

Adventure isn't hanging on a rope
off the side of a mountain…
Adventure is an attitude that we
must apply to the day-to-day
obstacles of life—facing new
challenges, seizing new
opportunities, testing our
resources against the unknown
and in the process, discovering
our own unique potential.

JOHN AMATT

Optimism is essential to achievement
and it is also the foundation of
courage and true progress.

NICHOLAS MURRAY BUTLER

optimism

An optimist is a person who sees a
green light everywhere, while the
pessimist sees only the red stoplight.

ALBERT SCHWEITZER

I am not bound to win, but I am bound to be true. I am not bound to succeed, but I am bound to live up to what light I have.

ABRAHAM LINCOLN

success

Forget about all the reasons why something may not work. You only need to find one good reason why it will.

DR. ROBERT ANTHONY

For success, attitude is equally as important as ability.

HARRY F. BANKS

steady

It is a curious thing in human experience, but to live through a period of stress and sorrow with another person creates a bond which nothing seems able to break.

ELEANOR ROOSEVELT

To be capable of steady friendship or lasting love, are the two greatest proofs, not only of goodness of heart, but of strength of mind.

WILLIAM HAZLITT

friendship

No birth certificate is issued when friendship is born. There is nothing tangible. There is just a feeling that your life is different and that your capacity to love and care has miraculously been enlarged without any effort on your part. It's like having a tiny apartment and somebody moves in with you. But instead of becoming cramped and crowded, the space expands, and you discover rooms you never knew you had until your friend moved in with you.

STEVE TESICH

17

Sometimes our light goes out but is blown into flame by another human being. Each of us owes deepest thanks to those who have rekindled this light.

ALBERT SCHWEITZER

loyal

Many a friendship—long, loyal, and self-sacrificing— rested at first upon no thicker a foundation than a kind word.

FREDERICK W. FABER

principles

Expedients are for the hour, but principles
are for the ages. Just because the rains
descend and the winds blow, we cannot
afford to build on shifting sands.

HENRY WARD BEECHER

growth

All of God's people are ordinary people who have been made extraordinary by the purpose He has given them.

OSWALD CHAMBERS

Growth is the only evidence of life.

JOHN HENRY NEWMAN

23

The paradox of courage
is that a man must be a
little careless of his life
even in order to keep it.

G.K. CHESTERTON

courage

The timid and fearful first failures dismay,
But the stout heart stays trying by night and by day.
He values his failures as lessons that teach
The one way to get to the goal he would reach.

EDGAR A. GUEST

Come out into the open,
into a clearing, and rest.

rest

Rest is not idleness, and
to lie sometimes on the
grass under trees on a
summer's day, listening to
the murmur of the water,
or watching the clouds
float across the sky, is by
no means a waste of time.

Rest when you're weary. Refresh and
renew yourself, your body, your mind,
your spirit. Then get back to work.

RALPH MARSTON

refresh

The best of all medicines is resting and fasting.

BENJAMIN FRANKLIN

Where there is life, there is hope.
Where there are hopes, there are
dreams. Where there are vivid
dreams repeated, they become
goals. Goals become the action
plans and game
plans that winners
dwell on in intricate
detail, knowing
that achievement
is almost automatic
when the goal becomes an inner
commitment. The response to the
challenges of life—purpose—is the
healing balm that enables each of
us to face up to adversity and strife.

DENNIS WAITLEY

Perseverance is a great element of success. If you only knock long enough and loud enough at the gate, you are sure to wake up somebody.

HENRY WADSWORTH LONGFELLOW

persevere

Four steps to achievement:
Plan Purposefully,
Prepare Prayerfully,
Proceed Positively,
and Pursue Persistently.

WILLIAM A. WARD

Every heart that has beat strongly and cheerfully
has left a hopeful impulse behind it in the world,
and bettered the tradition of mankind.

ROBERT LOUIS STEVENSON

hopeful

Never say you don't have enough time...You
have exactly the same number of hours per
day that were given to Helen Keller, Pasteur,
Michelangelo, Mother Teresa, Leonardo da Vinci,
Thomas Jefferson, and Albert Einstein.

AUTHOR UNKNOWN

If your heart is full of
love you will always
have something to give.

<small>AUTHOR UNKNOWN</small>

love

Love never fails.

<small>THE BOOK OF 1 CORINTHIANS</small>

Love doesn't make the world go 'round.
Love is what makes the ride worthwhile.

<small>FRANKLIN P. JONES</small>

Love looks through a telescope;
envy through a microscope.

JOSH BILLINGS

commitment

"True love" isn't so much
a dreamy feeling that you
have as it is an enduring
commitment to give
sacrificially—even, or
perhaps especially, when
you don't feel like it.

WILLIAM R. MATTOX JR.

And now these three remain: faith, hope and love. But the greatest of these is love.

THE BOOK OF 1 CORINTHIANS

wishes

You will find as you look back upon your life that the moments when you have truly lived are the moments when you have done things in the spirit of love.

HENRY DRUMMOND

Where there is great love, there are always wishes.

WILLA CATHER

Love accepts the trying things of
life without asking for explanations.
It trusts and is at rest.

<small>AMY CARMICHAEL</small>

trust

The supreme happiness in life is
the conviction that we are loved.

<small>VICTOR HUGO</small>

43

You can discover more about a person in an hour of play than in a year of conversation.

PLATO

It doesn't matter if you win or lose, it's how you play the game.

AUTHOR UNKNOWN

Work consists of whatever a body is obliged to do.
Play consists of whatever a body is not obliged to do.

MARK TWAIN

curiosity

The cure for boredom is curiosity.
There is no cure for curiosity.

DOROTHY PARKER

Man is most nearly himself when he
achieves the seriousness of a child at play.

HERACLITUS

invention

Necessity may be the mother of invention,
but play is certainly the father.

ROGER VON OECH

49

For the rest of my life I'm going to trust that God is always at work in all things, and give Him thanks long before my simplest prayers are answered.

NANCY PARKER BRUMMETT

serenity

God, give us grace to accept with serenity the things that cannot be changed, courage to change the things which should be changed, and the wisdom to distinguish one from the other.

REINHOLD NIEBUHR

Prayer changes things.

AUTHOR UNKNOWN

prayer

God of life, there are days when the burdens
we carry chafe our shoulders and wear us down;
when the road seems dreary and endless, the
skies gray and threatening; when our lives have
no music in them and our hearts are lonely,
and our souls have lost their courage. Flood
the path with light, we beseech you; turn our
eyes to where the skies are full of promise.

SAINT AUGUSTINE

Be not forgetful of prayer. Every time you pray, if your prayer is sincere, there will be a new feeling and a new meaning in it, which will give you fresh courage, and you will understand that prayer is an education.

FYODOR DOSTOEVSKY

My secret is simple. I pray.

MOTHER TERESA

sincere

Any concern too small to be turned into a prayer is too small to be made into a burden.

CORRIE TEN BOOM

Most people are about as happy
as they make up their minds to be.

ABRAHAM LINCOLN

happiness

Look to this day…Yesterday is already
a dream and tomorrow is only a vision.
But today, well-lived, makes every
yesterday a dream of happiness and
every tomorrow a vision of hope.

AUTHOR UNKNOWN

Happiness, not in another place but this place…
not for another hour, but this hour…

WALT WHITMAN

laughter

Laughter is day, and
sobriety is night; a
smile is the twilight
that hovers gently
between both, more
bewitching than either.

HENRY WARD BEECHER

Should we feel at times disheartened and discouraged, a confiding thought, a simple movement of heart towards God will renew our powers. Whatever He may demand of us, He will give us at the moment the strength and the courage that we need.

FRANCOIS FENELON

strength

I will see the goodness of the LORD
in the land of the living.
Wait for the LORD; be strong and take heart,
and wait for the Lord.

THE BOOK OF PSALMS

Failure is the
opportunity to
begin again more
intelligently.

HENRY FORD

opportunity

Dreams are renewable. No matter what our age
or condition, there are still untapped possibilities
within us and new beauty waiting to be born.

DR. DALE TURNER

grow

Unless you try to do
something beyond what
you have mastered, you
will never grow.

C.R. LAWTON